JESUS CHRIST FOR TODAY

WILLIAM BARCLAY

1908 Grand Avenue
Nashville, Tennessee 37203

Library of Congress Catalog Card Number: 73-86376
© 1973 by Tidings, 1908 Grand Avenue,
Nashville, Tenn. 37203
EV015B

CONTENTS

FOREWORD

I am very conscious of both the honor and the responsibility of being entrusted with the task of writing these studies on the life of Jesus as recorded in Luke's Gospel.

I have made no attempt to write a commentary in miniature. I have concentrated entirely on trying to find out what Luke says about the person and character of the evangelist, Jesus Christ, and about the task of evangelism.

It is almost impossible to rise from the study of Luke without having been made aware of the beauty and the width of the love of God in Jesus Christ. It is my hope and my prayer that these studies may enable the missioner to see his task clearly and to be more fully aware of his resources in Jesus Christ to go out upon it.

William Barclay

The University of Glasgow,
April 1973

FOR FURTHER STUDY

For those who wish to undertake further and more detailed study there is ample material. For those who can use the Greek text there are commentaries by A. B. Bruce in the *Expositor's Greek Testament;* by A. Plummer in the *International Critical Commentary;* and by J. M. Creed in the *Macmillan Commentary.*

There are commentaries on the English text by W. M. Manson in the *Moffatt Commentary;* by A. R. C. Leaney in the *A. and C. Black Commentary;* by G. B. Caird in the *Pelican Commentary;* by E. Earle Ellis in the *New Century Bible;* and by myself in the *Daily Study Bible.*

There is material about Luke's Gospel in general in the New Testament Introductions such as F. C. Grant's *The Gospels;* R. M. Grant's *Historical Introduction to the New Testament;* A. M. Hunter's *Introducing the New Testament;* E. B. Redlich's *Students' Introduction to the Synoptic Gospels;* E. F. Scott's *Literature of the New Testament;* Vincent Taylor's *The Gospels.*

There are special studies such as C. K. Barrett's *Luke the Historian in Recent Study* and H. Conzelmann's *The Theology of St. Luke.*

PREFACE

Scholars write books. Men learned and ignorant compose volumes on the New Testament. Christian evangelism is the subject of books innumerable. *Jesus Christ for Today* brings together all three, an author read for his scholarship the world around using a book of Scripture to base a strategy for evangelism. Doctor William Barclay, perhaps the most prolific Biblical scholar in the world, employs the Gospel of Luke to draw the guidelines for the Church's presentation of its Gospel.

There are evangelists, and evangelists. There are those who by gimmicks copied from the world of business promotion and fired by sheer animal heat pass among the faithful as "evangelists." Not seldom they evoke enthusiasm and draw crowds. They are successful in most every way — except in the furthering of genuine Christianity. Their message, except verbally, is not the Good News of the Faith. Professor Barclay has rightly seen that *Christian* evangelism is the word and way of Christ or it is not Christian. Further, he has realized that when the Church has achieved its greatest influence, even in a pagan world, it has been within the lines of the teaching and practice of Jesus.

What is the true message of our Lord? What methods did Jesus use to make his teachings effective? What is the true dynamic of the Christian life? Who make the best missioners of the Faith? Under what circumstances may the Gospel be rejected? What bearing does evangelism have on the social controversies that trouble our time? Does evangelism require a cross? With the sure pen of the established New Testament scholar Doctor Barclay expounds the truly Christian evangelist's answer to these crucial queries.

In these days there is the sound of a "going" in the tops of the mulberry trees, to use the Old Testament metaphor. There is a widely-shared conviction that unless there is a force sufficient to reverse present trends civilization cannot survive. "Evangelism" is becoming respectable again. We find it creeping back into the chairs of seminaries. Conferences and convocations are being organized for evangelistic endeavor. The call for repentance and belief in the Gospel is being heard again from the pulpit. Global movements like World Methodist Evangelism are picking up momentum. How fortunate in such an hour to have a Christian scholar of William Barclay's eminence to guide us!

I commend a reading of *Jesus Christ for Today* commensurate with its scholarly quality and faithfulness to the Christian enterprise.

Bishop F. Gerald Ensley
The United Methodist Church
Chairman of the World Methodist Council
Committee on Evangelism

1

THE MAN WHO WROTE THE GOSPEL

To study Luke's Gospel is to study what Renan called "the most beautiful book in the world." It may be called the earliest life of Jesus, and it is still one of the best. It is on record that a student asked James Denney to recommend a good life of Jesus, and that Denney answered: "Have you tried the one that Luke wrote?"

When we turn to the writings of Luke, we turn to the writings of the man who wrote more of the New Testament than any other of its authors. In the printed Revised Standard Version of the New Testament there are 552 pages. Luke's Gospel takes up 78 pages and Acts 71 pages, a total of 149 pages, which is to say that Luke wrote 27 per cent, more than a quarter, of the New Testament. Paul's letters take up 121 pages, which is quite a few less than the writings of Luke.

Of the three Synoptic Gospels Luke's is the most comprehensive. The total gospel material as contained in the material of the three Gospels can be divided into 172 sections, of which Luke contains 127, Matthew 114, and Mark 84. Of these sections 48 are found only in Luke, 22 only in Matthew and 5 only in Mark. This is to say that between one-third and one-quarter of the total gospel material is special to Luke. Luke has five miracles which are not in any other of the Gospels. He alone, for instance, has the raising of the widow's son at Nain (7:11-17); the healing of the ten lepers (17:11-19); (5:1-11, 13:10-17, 14:1-6). Luke alone, for instance, has the parable of the good Samaritan (10:29-37); the friend at midnight (11:5-8); the lost coin (15:8-10); the lost son (15:11-32); the rich man and Lazarus (16:19-31); the unjust judge (18:1-8); (7:40-43; 12:13-20; 13:6-9; 14:28-32; 16:1-9; 17:7-10; 18:9-14). It is only in Luke that we find the story of Zacchaeus (19:1-10); the trial before Herod (23:6-12); the story of the penitent thief (23:39-43); the walk to Emmaus (24:13-35). It

10

is easy to see what an immense debt we owe to Luke, and we can understand F. C. Grant when he says that, if he ever did have to choose which one Gospel he would choose to keep, if only one could be kept, it would be Luke.

We know very little about this Luke who was the largest contributor to the New Testament. Tradition says that he came from Antioch, that city in which the gospel was first preached to the Gentiles, and where the followers of Christ were first called Christians (Acts 11:19-26). In the New Testament itself there are only three direct references to him. In Philemon 24 Paul calls him one of his fellow-workers. From Colossians 4:11-15 we learn two important things about Luke. From the way in which the names are grouped in that passage we learn that Luke was a Gentile, for the list of Paul's Jewish friends stops at verse 11. It is an astonishing thing to think that the man who wrote more of the New Testament than anyone else was not a Jew but a Gentile. It may be that we find his Gospel specially attractive, because, being a Gentile, he speaks the kind of language which we speak, and thinks in the same way as we do. It is from verse 14 in this passage that we learn that Luke was a doctor. It is clear that Luke was a cultured Greek, because Luke 1:1-4 is the kind of introduction that Greek authors wrote to their books, and it is written in excellent Greek of which any Greek might be proud.

It may be that it was because he was a doctor that Luke wrote the kind of Gospel he did write. There is a saying that a clergyman sees men at their best, a lawyer sees men at their worst, and a doctor sees men as they really are. A good doctor can tell what is wrong with a man, and yet he is never repelled or disgusted by illness; his one desire is to help and to heal. That is to say, a good doctor sees men with clarity and with compassion, and that is certainly true of Luke.

The last reference to Luke is in 2 Timothy 4:11. As the last shades close around Paul only Luke the faithful is left with him. It may be that Luke paid a heavy price to be with Paul at the end. If we read Acts with care we see that for the most part the story is told in the *third* person plural — *they* did this, *they* did that. But sometimes it is told in the *first* person plural (Acts 16:10-17; 20:5-15; 21:1-18; 27:1 - 38:16). Chapter 27 begins with *we*, and it begins the story of how Paul under arrest made his last journey to Rome, there to be tried. It is natural to believe that, when Luke tells the story in the first person, he was there himself in person. This would mean that Luke accompanied Paul on his last journey to Rome, along with Aristarchus (Acts 27:1-2). How did Luke succeed in gaining permission to make that journey with Paul? It is very likely true that the law was that, when a man made a journey to Rome to be tried, he was allowed to be accompanied by two personal *slaves;* and it may well be that Luke and Aristarchus enrolled themselves as the slaves of Paul, in order to remain with him in the last days. Luke would become a slave rather than be parted from Paul.

Legend and tradition say three more things about Luke.

i. There is a tradition dating from the sixth century that Luke was a painter. The Empress Eudoxia is said to have found in Jerusalem a picture of Mary, the mother of Jesus, painted by Luke. And to this day there is in the Church of Saint Maria Maggiore in the Capella Paolina in Rome a picture which is claimed to be Luke's painting of Mary. This painting dates back at least to A. D. 847.

ii. An ancient Prologue to Luke's Gospel says of him that he died a natural death. "He never had a wife or children," it says, "and died at the age of seventy-four in Bithynia, full of the Holy Spirit."

iii. From the very earliest days Luke has been identified with, as the Authorized Version has it, the brother, whose praise is in the gospel throughout all the churches (2 Corinthians 8:18). The RSV calls him the brother who is famous through all the churches for his preaching of the gospel. It is in this way that he is commemorated in the Collect for St. Luke's Day:

> Almighty God, who called St. Luke the Physician, whose praise is in the gospel, to be an Evangelist and Physician of the soul; may it please thee, that by the wholesome medicine of the doctrine delivered by him, all the diseases of our souls may be healed; through the merits of thy Son Jesus Christ our Lord. Amen.

If this were indeed so, one very interesting possibility would emerge. Second Corinthians 12:18

could quite legitimately be translated: "I urged Titus to go and sent his brother with him." And if the brother of 2 Corinthians 8:18 is the same as the brother of 2 Corinthians 12:18, then Luke and Titus were brothers.

But these three extras are no more than traditions and legends.

Now let us see the distinguishing characteristics of this man Luke.

i. In the first place, Luke is an historian in a way that Matthew and Mark are not historians. Luke is the first man to see the Christian events against the background of world history. He uses no fewer than six historical events to date the emergence of John the Baptist on the stage of history (Luke 3:1-2). When he tells of the banishment from Rome which brought Aquila and Priscilla, he dates it as being in the reign of Claudius the Roman Emperor (Acts 18:2). For Luke the events of Christianity were not done in a corner; he sees them in the light of history. Further, Luke is the first *Church* historian. The other Gospel writers take the story up to the death and resurrection of Jesus — and leave it there. Luke goes on into the Church. It is quite true that

15

for Luke, as for all the New Testament thinkers, Jesus Christ was the end; in him the work of salvation is in one sense completed and done. But it is even truer to say that Luke saw Jesus as the *middle* of time. There was the long preparation of the Jewish nation. There was the actual coming of Jesus. But then there comes the time of the Church, the time of the Spirit, the time of salvation history, the taking out of the Gospel until all should be brought in. Luke alone sees the sweep of history, past, present, and future.

ii. This explains the great distinctive quality of Luke's Gospel, the characteristic which makes Luke's Gospel the perfect Gospel for an enterprise of evangelism. All four Gospels use the passage from Isaiah 40:3 as a foretelling of the coming of the herald of the Messiah (Matthew 3:3; Mark 1:1-2; John 1:23; Luke 3:4-6). But Luke is the only Gospel writer to continue the quotation to its last line — "and all flesh shall see the salvation of God." The furthest man on the widest circle — Luke wanted him. When Matthew is tracing the genealogy of Jesus, he traces it back to Abraham, the father of the Jewish race (Matthew 1:2); when Luke traces the genealogy he traces it back to Adam, the father of all mankind (Luke 3:38). When the aged Simeon took up the infant Jesus in his arms in the Temple court, he said of him that he would be "a light for revelation to the Gentiles, and for glory to thy people Israel" (Luke 2:32). For Luke there were no barriers to the love of God in Jesus Christ.

iii. Luke has a special place in his Gospel for the Samaritans. He alone has the parable of the Good Samaritan (10:30-37), and the story of the one grateful leper who was a Samaritan (17:11-19). Luke does not accept the belief that the Jews have no dealings with the Samaritans, when both are in Christ.

iv. Luke has an equally special place for the sinner and the outcast, and for the people with whom no respectable person would have anything to do. Only Luke tells of the penitent tax-collector, and of Zacchaeus who must have been the most hated man in Jericho (18:9-14; 19:2-20). Only Luke tells of the penitent thief on Calvary (23:39-43). Luke is quite sure that however bad a man is he cannot drift beyond God's love and care in Jesus Christ.

v. Luke has a special place for women in his

17

Gospel. True, the mother will always be queen within the family; but it was forbidden to educate Jewish women; that would be to cast pearls before swine. And the Jew in his morning prayer gave thanks that God had not made him a Gentile, a slave, or a woman. But in Luke we have Elizabeth, Mary the mother of Jesus in all her loveliness, Anna, the woman whose great love atoned for her sin, Mary Magdalene, Susanna and Joanna, Martha and Mary, the widow with the two mites which were the greatest offering of all (1:5, 24-27, 58; 1:26-56; 2:36-38; 7:36-50; 8:2; 10:38-41; 21:1-4). They too had their place within the Kingdom.

If we wish to have our passion for the souls of men kindled again, we cannot go to a better flame than the flame of Luke's universal love.

For Discussion

1. What Guidance has Luke's Gospel to give about the Christian attitude to apartheid and to racialism?

2. Luke sees Jesus as the middle of time. Compare the following two sayings as they are transmitted by the three Synoptic Gospel writers:

    (a) Matthew 16:28; Mark 9:1; Luke 9:27.
    (b) Matthew 26:63-64; Mark 14:61-62; Luke 22:67-69.

It is clear that the thought of the Second Coming is less prominent in Luke. What place is there for the doctrine of the Second Coming today?

3. Luke was a doctor and an evangelist. Do you think that there ought to be a closer connection between religion and medicine, between the church and the hospital, between the doctor of medicine and the minister of religion?

Notes

2

THE MOMENT, THE MESSAGE, AND THE METHOD

The success of any campaign will very largely depend on the choice of the right moment at which to launch out upon it.

For Jesus the years were passing. He was thirty (Luke 3:23), and he was known quite simply as the carpenter of Nazareth (Mark 6:3). But with the emergence of John the Baptizer, Jesus knew that the hour had struck. What was special about John?

(a) One of the standard beliefs of Judaism was that, before the Messiah came, Elijah would come back to announce his coming and to be his herald (Malachi 3:1; 4:5). The description of John the Baptizer (Mark 1:6; Matthew 3:4) corresponds exactly to the description of Elijah in the Old

Testament (2 Kings 1:8). To Jesus it was clear that John was the herald of the Kingdom which he himself had come to inaugurate.

(b) It was one of the great regrets of the Jews that for the last four hundred years before the coming of Jesus the authentic voice of prophecy had been silent. "There is no longer any prophet" (Psalm 74:9). But simply to listen to John was to be sure that the voice of prophecy was speaking again.

(c) But there was one unique feature about the ministry of John. John was inviting the Jews to come to the Jordan to be baptized in repentance of their sins, and they were coming in their crowds (Luke 3:3; Mark 1:5). It was the simple fact that no one before John had ever called upon *Jews* to be baptized, and, if he had, the Jews would have refused the summons. For, as the Jews had hitherto seen it, baptism was for the heathen; certainly if a gentile became a proselyte, he had to be baptized. But the Jews, so they believed, because of their connection with Abraham (Luke 3:8) were in a specially privileged position and needed none of these things. At that moment a sense of sin had swept over the people;

they realized their need as never before. So Jesus came too — not that he needed repentance, for he had no sin, but in order to identify himself with his people in their search for God. Jesus' consent to his baptism was proof of his complete identification with men.

At the baptism something happened—"the Holy Spirit descended upon him" (Luke 3:22). Herein was the equipment of Jesus for his task. In the Old Testament there were men upon whom the Spirit had come — Gideon (Judges 6:34); Jephthah (Judges 11:29); Samson (Judges 14:6; 14:19; 15:14). But in the case of the Old Testament heroes the coming of the Spirit upon them was a temporary and abnormal phenomenon, which made them capable of one big moment and then left them. In the case of Jesus the equipment of the Spirit was permanent. In the Spirit of God he lived and moved and had his being.

So to Jesus the moment of action had come; the time of mission was there. But once a man has decided that the moment to embark on the campaign has come, he must then go on and decide how to fight it. That is what Jesus did in his temptations (Luke 4:1-12). It must be remembered that the Greek word for *to tempt* is *peirezein,* which means rather *to test* than *to tempt.* In Genesis 22:1, the beginning of the story of Abraham's consent to sacrifice Isaac — a consent which did not in the end become necessary — the older translations had it: "God did *tempt* Abraham." Obviously God never tried to seduce any man into sin, and correctly the newer translations have: "God tested Abraham." So the *temptations* of Jesus are the *testing* of Jesus. Temptation is not something designed to make us fall; it is something out of which we are meant to emerge stronger, tested, tried like gold in the fire.

Jesus was faced by three tests. First, the Tempter urged him to turn the stones into bread. The stones in the desert were exactly the shape of little rolls of bread. Here was a double temptation. It was a temptation to use his powers selfishly, for his own sake — which Jesus never did. It was a temptation to use his powers to give people material gifts, to bribe them to follow him by giving them bread. Make no mistake — Jesus *was* interested that the hungry should eat; but there was a hunger of the soul that all the material gifts

24

in the world could not satisfy, which only God and his word could fill. And that is a truth which is very valid for an age which "never had it so good," and at the same time has never had it so lawless, so violent, so immoral.

Second, the Tempter made the sight of the kingdoms of the world pass Jesus' mind's eye, and said to Jesus that, if Jesus would only worship him, all those things would be his. This is the temptation to compromise. The Tempter was saying: "Don't pitch your demands quite so high. Do a deal with me." But Jesus' answer is that God is God and God alone must be served. Again, there is a truth very valid for an age which has done everything possible to obliterate the difference between the church and the world — even to talking about religionless Christianity.

Third, there was from the Temple Pinnacle to the Kedron Valley below a sheer dizzying drop of four hundred feet. "Jump," said the Tempter, "and float down unhurt, and they will believe in you." "No," said Jesus, "you must never see how far you can go with God and get away with it." Here was the temptation to sensationalism, and sensationalism is always a losing game, for today's

25

sensation is tomorrow's common-place. Again, here is a truth for an age which sometimes attempts Christianity by gimmick.

So Jesus was equipped for his task and settled his method, and then he preached. His message is in Luke 4:16-24 — good news to the poor, release for the captives, sight for the blind, liberty for the oppressed. Compare the message of Jesus with the message of John. "The axe is laid to the root of the trees; every tree therefore that does not bear good fruit is cut down and thrown into the fire . . . His winnowing fork is in his hand, to clear his threshing floor, and to gather the wheat into his granary, but the chaff he will burn with unquenchable fire." (Luke 3:9-17) No one could ever call John's message a gospel, good news; it was the terrifying announcement of doom. On the other hand the message of Jesus was the promise of rescue for the captive, wealth for the poor, sight for the blind, freedom for those who are oppressed. The message of Jesus was characteristically a gospel, good news. In one of William Faulkner's novels a father says to his son: "I'll beat the love of God into you." He did not, because he could not.

The initial message of Jesus, as Luke has it, is the proof that Jesus believed that it is easier to love a man to God than it is to threaten him to God. The message of John was the message of the threat; the message of Jesus was the message of the promise. John tried to win men by the fear of hell; Jesus tried to win them by the love of God.

So then, if we are to set out on a campaign of evangelism for Jesus Christ we need the prophetic voice in which God unmistakably speaks again; the complete identification with the people whom we wish to win; the gift of the Spirit to fit us for the task. We need to avoid anything in the nature of the bribe to enter the Church. Compromise with the world in the end wins not sympathy but contempt, for what use is religion if it does no more than make a man the same as the world? Sensationalism follows the law of diminishing returns, for today's nine days' wonder becomes tomorrow's commonplace. And above all we have to remember that the greatest evangelistic force in the world is the love of God in Jesus Christ the crucified.

For Discussion

1. What does it mean to identify oneself with sinners?
2. What ought to be the difference between the Christian and the non-Christian?
3. How can the social gospel be given its full place, but no more than its place?
4. In our evangelism how can we hold the balance between the proclamation of the love and of the wrath of God?

THE MOMENT, THE MESSAGE, AND THE METHOD

Notes

3

THE REJECTION OF THE MESSAGE

We know well that the mission of Jesus ended in the rejection of himself and of his message. Let us go through Luke's Gospel and trace the various reasons why men rejected Jesus and ended by nailing him to a cross.

i. Signs of what was to happen came very soon. When Jesus went to Nazareth, his home town, and brought God's offer to the people there, "they rose up and put him out of the city, and led him to the brow of the hill on which their city was built, that they might throw him down headlong" (Luke 4:16-30; Mark 6:1-6; Matthew 13:53-58).

What was the matter? What made them resent him so much that they wanted to throw him violently out of their city? "Isn't this Joseph's son?" they said. "Wasn't he the village carpenter? Don't we know his mother and his brothers and his sisters?" Quite simply, they refused to believe that the village boy they had known so well had any right to talk like that. The curious thing about men is that they will often take calmly from a stranger what they will not accept from one of their own people. It may be that there will be times when we will need to have a care not to resist the word of God, because it is being spoken by some one whom we think we know too well.

ii. But there were far deeper causes of cleavage than that. They resented it, because he had come to convey God's forgiveness to men, and said so (Luke 5:17-26; Mark 2:1-12; Matthew 9:2-8). The first thing that Jesus said to the man who was let down through the roof before him was: "Your sins are forgiven."

When we read a story like that, we have to remember that in New Testament times sin and suffering were inextricably connected. If a man suffered, then so they believed, quite certainly he had sinned; and if he sinned, so they believed, quite certainly he would suffer. The result was that in those days many people suffered from diseases which were far more psychological than

31

physical. They knew that they had sinned, and they thought themselves into illness or paralysis. The mind can affect the body. To take a simple example, we may well wake up with a headache or a heavy cold on a day when we have an engagement we do not wish to face, or a task we do not wish to do. Our mind is acting on our body, to provide us with a defence mechanism against doing the things we do not want to do. Jesus knew this, and he knew that, if ever this poor man was to be cured, he must first be sure he was forgiven. We do not now connect sin and suffering in this cast iron way, but it is still true that a sense of being forgiven by God exhilarates a man in body and in soul.

iii. The orthodox good people resented the company that Jesus kept. He was the friend of tax collectors and sinners; he would sit and eat and talk with those with whom no respectable person would have anything to do. A prostitute's broken-hearted gratitude for her discovery what real love means did not embarrass him at all (Luke 5:29-32; 7:34-39; 15:1).

He who would follow the evangelism of Jesus always has to go where the need is deepest. In

Kipling's poem Mulholland on the cattle boat made the promise that, if in the moment of crisis God saved his life, he would from that time serve God. God did save him, and Mulholland was ready to keep his bargain. But his idea was to serve God "handsome and out of the wet." But God told him: "Back you go to the cattle boats and preach my gospel there." C. T. Studd used to have a four-line jingle:

> Some wish to preach within the sound
> > Of church or chapel bell;
> I want to run a rescue shop
> > Within a yard of hell.

But two things have to be said and said forcibly. First, no matter to whom we go, we must never go as those who are doing the other person a favor. We must never be the good ones going to the bad ones, the saved going to the damned. Jesus identified himself with sinners in their search for God and for forgiveness. As it has been put, we must be like one hungry man telling another hungry man where to find bread. There must be no such thing as evangelical slumming. And second, it must never be thought that the sinners are all at the one end of the scale. Men

33

need God, and men defy God, in the fashionable hotel just as much as in the cheap rooming house. The splendidly dressed lady may be just as much in need of the grace of God as the drab street-walker. There is every bit as much need for evangelism at the top end of the social scale as at the bottom.

iv. The orthodox people resented Jesus because he loved people more than he loved the law. The Jews had deified the law, and especially the oral law. The law itself, as it is presented in the Ten Commandments, is a series of great wide principles which we must ourselves apply. The Jewish Scribes and Rabbis and Pharisees broke the principles down into thousands and thousands of petty regulations to try to give a man a rule for every possible situation in life. The command said that a man must not work on the Sabbath (Exodus 20:8-11). But what is work? Thirty-nine classifications of work were worked out. One classification was carrying a burden. But what is a burden? If a man lifted his child on the Sabbath day, was he carrying a burden? Not unless the child had a stone in his hand. But what is a stone? Anything big enough to throw at a bird. Is a woman carrying a burden if she wears some false hair, or a man when he wears dentures? This to the legalistic Jew was religion. Keeping these petty commands was pleasing God.

One of the works forbidden on the Sabbath was healing. Measures could be taken to keep a patient from getting worse but not to make him better. A plain bandage might be put on a wound, but not a bandage with ointment. Jesus walked straight through this law and healed the sick again and again (Luke 6:6-11; 13:10-17; 14:1-6), and the Jewish legalists quite honestly and sincerely thought that he was a bad man and a threat to all morality.

The trouble with these people was that they loved a system more than they loved people; the characteristic of Jesus was that he would allow no system to stop him helping the man who needs help at any time. And in the end they killed him for this, because they loved their systems more than they loved God.

This danger is always here. There are some people who still act as if it were more important to be a Methodist, an Anglican, a Presbyterian, a Congregationalist, a Baptist, a Roman Catholic than it is to be a Christian. The only church that a Christian can belong to is the Church of Jesus Christ. Evangelism must never be propaganda for a particular church, still less for a particular congregation; it must be propaganda for Jesus Christ. Of course we will wish to welcome a man into a congregation — but to introduce him, not to a system, but to Christ.

v. The orthodox resented Jesus because he attached vested interests. He cleansed the Temple courts; and the shops and booths belonged to the family of Annas. No wonder Annas gloated over the arrest of this young Galilean. Certain things we note. So very often the chief priests are referred to as Jesus' implacable enemies (Luke 19:47; 20:19-20; 22:21). The priests were all Sadducees; the Sadducees were the wealthy, worldly aristocracy. And they were the collaborators with the Romans. All they wanted was to preserve their status and their money. The one thing they feared was disturbance, and the last thing they wanted was a Messiah.

In the examination of Jesus the charge made against him was blasphemy (Luke 22:67; Mark 14:61-64; Matthew 26:62-66). *But that was not*

the charge on which they brought him to Pilate.
They knew that Pilate would not listen to such a
charge, so they charged him with being a political
revolutionary — and they knew it was a lie (Luke
23:1-5). He had attacked their vested interests;
he must go.

If we read the Old Testament regulations, we
see the enormous perquisites the priests had. Part
of the almost every sacrifice went to them (Le-
viticus 2:3-10; 6:16, 26, 29; 7:6-10; 7:31-36).
They lived the lushest of lives. Ordinary people
were luck if they ate meat once a week; the priests
suffered from an occupational disease which came
from eating too much meat. There were so many
of them that their actual temple service required
only two weeks in the year. They lived in a lux-
urious idleness — and if Jesus was right that God
wanted mercy and not sacrifice (Matthew 9:13),
their good time was finished. Therefore, crucify
him!

Men still reject Jesus, and we will find in Luke's
analysis of the situation the difficulties which still
have to be faced, and, without realizing them, we
cannot overcome them.

For Discussion

1. Where do you think evangelism is more difficult — at the top or the bottom of the social
   scale? Do you think that the evangelist will
   need different methods and techniques for
   the different levels of society? If you do think
   so, work out the variations which will be
   needed.
2. What is the connection between evangelism
   and ecumenicity? How can we avoid compe-
   tition between the denominations? How can
   we avoid conflict between "brands" of theology? Is it possible for the theological liberal
   and conservative, and radical and fundamen-
   talist to work together in evangelism?
3. Are there any vested interests with which
   evangelism might clash today?

THE REJECTION OF THE MESSAGE

Notes

4

THE MISSIONERS OF THE KING

In any study the primary aim of which is the preparation for evangelism it is of primary importance to study the missioners whom Jesus sent out, and the task that was laid upon them. In Luke's Gospel there are two passages which are of special importance, the passage which tells of the sending out of the Twelve (Luke 9:1-6) and the passage which tells of the sending out of the Seventy-two (Luke 10:1-20). We shall take these two passages together to try to get a picture of the missioner and his task.

Before we come to the passages themselves, let us look at the way in which the missioners are described. In Luke 6:13 it is said that Jesus called them *apostles*. In Greek the word *apostolos* means *one who is sent*. In Greek the word can mean an ambassador, and in Hebrew its equivalent can mean an emissary of the Sanhedrin. But the word has one special characteristic. An *apostolos,* an apostle, was not sent out in his own authority; he bore with him and upon him all the authority of him who sent him. As an ambassador speaks not for himself but for his country, an apostle speaks not for himself but for his sender. This then means that the missioner, the apostle of Jesus, speaks not for himself but for Jesus, and goes forth not in his own authority, but clad with the authority of the Lord who sends him.

In Matthew the missioners are called *disciples* (Matthew 10:1). The word *disciple* means a *learner.* So the Christian missioner must continually be learning about Jesus. We cannot teach what we have not learned, and, if we lived and learned for a thousand lives, we would never reach the end of the unsearchable riches of Christ. Therefore the missioner of Christ must ever be learning more of his Lord.

In Mark 3:14 it is said that Jesus chose his men that they might be with him and that he might send them out. The missioner must be with Jesus before he goes out for Jesus. We can never

introduce anyone to someone we do not ourselves
know. The missioner must know the Lord before
he can bring others to the Lord. He must go out
to men from the presence of Jesus. To put it another way, there can be no preaching without
prayer.

i. In Luke's Gospel the tasks of the missioners
are clearly laid down. They are to exorcise de-
mons; they are to heal the sick; they are to preach
the Kingdom (Luke 9:1-2; 10:8, 17). There is
something curiously modern here, something
which the most modern medicine would fully
approve and understand.

Monroe Peaston in *Personal Living* gives us the
outline of the beliefs and practices of Paul Tournier, one of the greatest of modern physicians.
Tournier has one basic belief — all healing must
be the healing of the whole man, the man in his
entirety. It must therefore combine medical
knowledge, psychological understanding and religious insight. This is precisely what Jesus was
demanding. The missioner must heal — he must
cure the body; the missioner must exorcise de-
mons — he must cure the patient psychologically;

he must preach the Kingdom — he must bring religious insight to the heart and soul.

Tournier takes certain examples. Here is a man with digestive troubles. Medical knowledge must examine him and find what is physically wrong. But this man is in fact being unfaithful to his wife and is living in tension. Psychological technique must persuade him to admit and to face this and to realize the damage it is doing to him. Then to the man there must be brought grace, the dynamic, the power of Jesus Christ that he may remake his life. Medicine, psychology, religion have joined hands to rescue this man — just as Jesus commanded.

This is the true evangelism. Evangelism must be far more than a mass 'revival' meeting with a call to come forward to be saved. Then may be the beginning of the process — but it is only the beginning. The true Christian evangelist must rescue, through Christ, the man from his spiritual dilemma, cleanse his mind, lift up his heart, heal his body. It may well be too much to say that, if evangelism is going to begin and end with the mass meeting, it would be better not to begin.

ii. In Luke's Gospel the work of the missioner

is strangely personal. It is the missioner and the *house* that are spoken of (Luke 9:4, 10:5-7). There is nothing about the mass meeting or about any other kind of meeting. It is a person to person encounter. Tournier says that at least in certain cases his method would be simply to start by talking about Jesus Christ, about forgiveness and about the peace that comes from giving oneself to him.

Tournier holds that each person has an inner core, and round that core he builds his disguises and defenses, that each of us presents to the world a personage, while deep down there is a *person*. It is to the person we must get. For that we do not need information about people so much as we need communion with them. Tournier says that in a conversation with a person, "there suddenly awakens within me the certainty that I am no longer learning, but understanding. . . . It is not the sum of what I have learned. It is a light which has suddenly burst forth from our personal contact." It is a moment of mutual "transparency". This is real evangelism.

I knew a psychiatrist who thought nothing of spending two hundred hours on the one patient;

I knew a minister who sent postcards to the people he intended to visit on any given evening, saying that he would arrive at 7:40 and leave at 7:50 P.M. — ten minutes per house. What a lesson the psychiatrist could teach the clergyman!

We must never connect evangelism only with the mass meeting, the eloquent appeal and nothing more. Real evangelism, as Jesus saw it, meant the entry to the home, the sitting down beside the person, the opening of heart to heart, the search for communion, for the moment of transparency, the moment when Jesus really comes.

iii. In Luke's Gospel there are certain personal things said about the evangelist.

(a) He is sent out like a lamb in the midst of wolves (Luke 10:3). The mark of the evangelist is innocence rather than cleverness, simplicity rather than sophistication. The simpler the evangelist is the more easily he will get beside the other person. The cleverer he seems to be, the more difficult it will be, for people fear and suspect the expert. The knowledge must be there but it must be cloaked in humility.

(b) He is to travel light. Luke's Gospel's description of the missioner of Christ stresses the

fact that his possessions in this world are reduced
to a bare minimum (Luke 9:3, 10:4). Francis
of Asissi's rule for his friars was based on three
texts — the text which orders the missioner to take
nothing with him (Matthew 10:9, 10); the text
which bids the man who would be perfect to sell
all that he has and to give to the poor (Matthew
19:21); the text which bids the Christian to deny
himself, to take up his cross and to follow his
Master (Matthew 16:24). We need not stop to
argue whether or not this applies literally to all
Christians; the one thing we can say without
doubt is that the success of any mission is not
due to the lavishness of its material resources, the
size of its bank balance, the excellence of its
technical equipment with electric typewriters and
addressographs and card indexes and files. These
things have their place, but the one thing that
matters above all is the total commitment of the
missioner to Jesus Christ.

(c) The missioner is bidden to salute no one
on the road (Luke 10:4). In Palestine when two
travellers met, the likelihood was that they would
first stand and then sit and talk for a long, long
time about mutual acquaintances and village

gossip and the like. Time in the East is something which is of no value. The Christian missoner is not being urged to discourtesy; but he is being urged to remember that time is short and he must not be talking when he should be acting. The social decencies are necessary, but they must not infringe on the time for action. The pleasantries of a banquet and the arguments of a committee can both be evasions of the duty of action.

iv. It is of interest and importance to note that in Luke's Gospel the metaphor of the harvest is used, and that the missoner is likened to the reaper (Luke 10:2). This takes our thoughts straight to the parable of the sower (Luke 8:4-8). We often take that parable to mean that the fate of the seed depends on the ground into which it is sown, and that point may well be there. But there is no doubt what the real point is of the parable. The parable culminates in the description of the good seed with the abundant yield. And its lesson certainly is — even if some seed is lost on the path, through the birds, in the shallow ground, that does not affect the ultimate fact that *the harvest is sure*. Jesus told this parable at a time when things seemed to be going wrong, when the opposition was growing, and when the orthodox authorities were massing against Jesus, and when inevitably the disciples were growing discouraged. In it Jesus says: "No farmer would refuse to sow because he knows that some seed will be lost. He knows that some seed will be lost, but he also knows that the harvest is sure." An over-cautious worry and a too easy discouragement are to be avoided. The Preacher writes: "He who observes the wind will not sow; and he who regards the clouds will not reap." (Ecclesiastes 11:4) Let the missioner remember that of course there is a risk, and of course there are failures, but nonetheless the harvest is sure.

v. Luke's Gospel reminds us that there is a grave responsibility on those who hear the message and reject it (Luke 9:5; 10:10-16). When the Jew left a heathen city, into which he had had to go, he shook from his sandals the very last particle of dust, to show that he left heathenism behind him. The place that would not receive the Gospel was to be treated as a heathen city.

It must always be remembered that responsibility is the other side of privilege. It is a privilege to have received the offer of the Gospel; the man who refuses the offer will not be held guiltless. Better never to have heard than to have heard and refused.

vi. One last point emerges from Luke's account of the commission of the missioner. The missioners were to go where Jesus was to follow (Luke 10:1). Their one aim was to prepare men to receive Jesus Christ. For themselves they must seek no prominence; for themselves they must expect neither praise, nor thanks, nor even notice. They must be prepared to efface themselves, to fade from the picture, and to leave men face to face with Jesus Christ.

Such is the picture of the missioner of the King, and such must be the pattern of the modern evangelist.

For Discussion

1. What preparations both of the evangelist and of the methods of our evangelism ought we to make before we begin our campaign?

2. What is the part of the mass meeting, and what is the part of face to face, person to person communication in evangelism? What special training does the missioner need for person to person evangelism?

3. What steps should be taken to insure the after-care of those who in and through a campaign have been attracted to Jesus?

Notes

5

THE DYNAMIC OF THE CHRISTIAN LIFE

If an author has at his disposal more material than he can possibly include, nothing tells us so much about him as that which he chooses to include and that which he chooses to omit.

It was that way with Luke, as it must have been with most ancient writers. Luke wrote before the days of paper, of printing and of the book. In his day books were written on papyrus, which was a substance made of the pith of papyrus bulrush. The pith was cut into strips and then pressured together, into a material resembling brown paper. It was made in sheets measuring about ten inches by eight. It was not a cheap material; the cheapest papyrus cost about two new pence per sheet (about 10-25 cents), and the best papyrus would cost anything up to eight new pence a sheet. Papyrus was an expensive substance which a writer would use as economically as possible. The book form of binding had not yet emerged when Luke wrote. The sheets were joined side by side to form a long strip, on which the writing was in narrow columns about two and a half inches wide. The strip was then rolled up to form a roll. When it was read, it was held in the left hand, unrolled with the right, and rolled up again with the left hand as it was read. Obviously the papyrus roll was an unwieldy thing; and the maximum usable roll was about thirty feet long. Nowadays a book may be expanded to almost any length; printing and paper are, comparatively speaking, cheap; but it was not until the tenth century that paper arrived in the west and not till the fifteenth century that printing was invented. So then a writer like Luke was strictly limited, both by the price and the form of his material. Of necessity he had to be selective, and clearly what he selects will give evidence of what he regards as important.

It is therefore of great interest that there are seven occasions when Luke alone of the Gospel writers shows us Jesus at prayer. The occasions are: at his baptism; before the first conflict with the Jewish authorities; before the choosing of the Twelve; before the first confession of Peter and the prediction of his sufferings and death; at the Transfiguration; before he taught his disciples to pray; and twice on the Cross (3:21; 5:16; 6:12; 9:18; 9:29; 11:1; 23:34; 23:46). Further, it is Luke alone who gives us the two prayer parables, the parable of the friend at midnight (11:5-8), and the parable of the unjust judge (18:1-8). It is clear that Luke is out to show us the place of prayer in the life of Jesus, and therefore the place of prayer in our own life.

Repeatedly Luke shows us Jesus going out to the wilderness or up to the hillside to pray (5:16; 6:12; 9:28). He withdrew to the wilderness, or went out to the hill, and prayed. Once a friend said to that great preacher Alexander Whyte: "You preached today as if you had come straight from the presence." And Whyte answered softly: "Perhaps I did." Jesus always came from the presence of God into the presence of men. He knew that before he faced the crowds he had to be alone. When her persecutors told Joan of Arc that she stood alone and that she was forsaken by all, she answered: "It is better to be alone with God. His friendship will not fail me, nor his counsel, nor his love. In his strength I will dare and dare and dare, until I die." Jesus too knew the necessity of being alone with God. Joan always talked about "her voices." The Dauphin complained that he never heard such "voices." Joan's answer was that he never stood quiet and still in the twilight, listening to the thrilling of the bells in the evening air, after they had stopped ringing. If he had done that, he would have heard. The sole reason why we so often do not hear the voice of God is that we do not listen; we do not stand still in the silence and give him a chance to speak. He who would tell men of Christ, must like Jesus first listen to God, and to listen to God he must be still. Let us see then how Jesus used prayer.

i. He prayed in the moment of decision, for the baptism was for him the moment when he decided that his work must begin (3:21). It must be true of the follower of Jesus that he never does anything without seeking the advice and the guidance of God. "Lord, what do you want me to do?" is the Christian's continual question (Acts 22:10).

ii. He prayed before the moment of conflict
(5:16). He knew he was on a collision course
with the establishment, with the orthodox lead-
ers of Judaism, and before the conflict he prayed.
It will happen to all of us that we will meet
with opposition; it will happen to all of us that
there comes the possibility of conflict. We shall
only be able to distinguish quarreling and disput-
ing from standing for principle and the right when
we lay the issue before God. In the sight of God
it will be quite clear what is principle and what
is prejudice, what is petty squabbling and what
is standing for the right, when it is right to fight
and when it is right to yield in peace. All summons to conflict must be tested by the presence of
God.

iii. He prayed all night before he chose his
men (6:12). We do well to pray to God before
we enter into friendship and commitment with
men. We shall have to choose our allies and only
as we see all issues and all men in the light of
God shall we choose correctly. When Charles
Kingsley thought of the dynamic of his life
towards truth and beauty, he explained it by
thinking of the influence of F. D. Maurice, and

so saying: "I had a friend." When Robert Burns was thinking of his ruined life, he remembered the man whom in his youth he had met when he went to learn flax-dressing in Irvine, and said of him: "His friendship did me a mischief." The friend who saves and the friend who ruins — the test is to take friendship, as Jesus did, to the verdict of God.

iv. He prayed before the moment of truth (9:18). He prayed in that time when he asked his disciples if they had discovered who he was, and before that moment when he told them plainly that ahead there lay nothing but suffering and death — with resurrection at the end of it (9:18-22). Jesus prayed in that moment when he knew that he must face truth himself and must help others to face it. The vision to face the truth, the honesty to accept the truth, the courage to tell the truth all come to us in the presence of God.

v. He prayed in the presence of death; he prayed on the Cross (23:34; 23:46). He prayed for forgiveness for his enemies, for, however much men might hate him and hurt him, Jesus would go to God with bitterness to no man. One of the surest ways of living at peace with men is to pray for them, for somehow or other we cannot hate a man we pray for. Jesus' final prayer was: "Father, into thy hands I commit my spirit" (23:46). That is Psalm 31:5 with the word Father added, and it was the prayer which every Jewish mother taught her child to pray before he slept. Jesus died with a child's goodnight prayer of trust on his lips. But to the words of the Psalm, as we saw, Jesus added one word — Father. That is the word he used in Gethsemane (22:42), and as Mark tells it the actual word he used was Abba (Mark 14:36), and that is the word by which we too can address God (Romans 8:15, Galatians 4:6). No one on earth had used this word to God before. It is not just Father. It was and is the word by which the little Jewish child addressed his father in the home circle — Daddy. It was with the intimacy and the trust like that that Jesus prayed — and so may we.

vi. I think that we can say that it was Jesus' example of prayer that made others wish to pray. It was when he was praying that his disciples came to him and asked him to teach them to pray (11:1). They had seen what prayer had done for him; they had seen what prayer had done for John; and they too wanted to pray. True prayer can bring to life a strength and beauty which move men more than any sermons. Only he who has the secret of the presence can make others desire the secret of presence too.

vii. Two things came to Jesus in prayer. The Spirit came to him in prayer at his baptism (3:21), and the vision came to him at his Transfiguration (9:29). The Spirit will only come when we learn the wise passivity which in silence waits and accepts. At the Transfiguration Jesus saw in his vision Moses the supreme lawgiver and Elijah the supreme prophet, and the supreme men of God of the past urged him to go on. In prayer we become one with the unseen cloud of witness who compass us about. In prayer the inspiration of the past gives us strength for the future.

viii. Jesus prayed for his friends when he knew they were going to be in trouble; he prayed for Peter when he knew that Peter's faith was going to be tested to the limit and beyond. (22:31-32). If we love our friends, we will pray for our friends, as Jesus did for his — and especially when they are in trouble.

iv. Lastly, Jesus told the two prayer parables,

the parable of the friend at midnight and the
parable of the unjust judge (11:5-8, 18:1-8).
There are no two parables in the Gospels which
are more misunderstood and misused. A parable
is something which is laid beside something else,
so that by the comparison the real meaning of the
thing may be elucidated. In most cases the comparison is made because the two things resemble
one another; but in these two parables the comparison depends on contrast, not on resemblance.
The one parable tells of a householder who was
very unwilling to get out of bed to give his friend
the bread he needed, but who was finally coerced
into getting up by his friend's shameless persistence in knocking at the door. The other parable tells of a notoriously unjust judge who was
compelled in the end to render justice because of
the sheer persistence of a widow woman, a persistence which finally wore him down.

Often these parables are used to teach the lesson of persistence in prayer, as if to say that you
will get what you want if you batter at God long
enough. But these two parables do not *compare*
God to an unwilling friend or an unjust judge;
they *contrast* him with such people. They say: "If

a churlish and unwilling householder can finally be coerced into giving a friend bread, if an unjust judge can finally be coerced into giving a widow justice, *how much more* will God your loving father give you what you need." This is exactly what Luke goes on to say: "If you then, who are evil, know how to give good gifts to your children, *how much more* will the heavenly Father give the Holy Spirit to those who ask him!" (11:9-13) These parables tell us, not that God's gifts have to be extracted by wearing down God's resistance, but that God is more willing to give than we are to ask.

Luke's Gospel is the Gospel of prayer, and is the Gospel for the missioner of Jesus, who must also be a man of prayer.

For Discussion

1. If the two prayer parables, the parable of the friend at midnight and the parable of the unjust judge, really teach that God does not need to be coerced into answering prayer, what are we to say about all night prayer meetings, and about organizing large numbers of people to pray for the same thing? Do we really think that the length of prayer and the amount of prayer are going to move God to act in some special way? Do we really think that we can, as it were, put pressure on God?

2. What is the relationship between our prayers and our efforts?

3. What things are right to pray for, and what things are wrong to pray for? Is it true to say that sometimes in prayer we try to make use of God?

THE DYNAMIC OF THE CHRISTIAN LIFE

Notes

6

PARABLES OF LIFE

In our last study we began by remembering that the circumstances in which an ancient author worked demanded that he should be selective, and we saw that that which he chooses to include and that which he chooses to omit combine to give an insight into his own faith, and into the notes which for him were the dominant tones of Christianity.

One of the most valuable things about Luke is that he gives us thirteen of Jesus' stories which are not found in any other Gospel. These were the stories which made the greatest impression on Luke; these were the stories which specially lodged in his memory. So if we look at these stories, we will be entitled to believe that they specially tell us what Christianity meant to Luke.

The stories which belong particularly to Luke are the following parables: the two debtors (7:40-43); the good Samaritan (10:29-37); the friend at midnight (11:5-8); the rich fool (12:13-20); the barren fig tree (13:6-9); the rash builder and the reckless king (14:28-32); the lost coin (15:8-10); the lost son (15:11-32); the unjust steward (16:1-9); the rich man and Lazarus (16:19-31); the farmer and the servant (17:7-10); the unjust judge (18:1-8); the Pharisee and the tax collector (18:9-14). When we examine these stories, we find that each one of them confronts the Christian missioner with a question which he must face and answer. Let us look at these stories, and let us face their questions.

i. Luke chooses two stories to drive home the truth that *people matter,* that concern for others is the very essence of the Christian life, that nothing can take the place of caring.

This is what the parable of the good Samaritan says (10:29-37). The priest and the Levite were so-called holy men, servants of God in the conventional sense of the term; the Samaritan was an outcast, some one with whom no respectable Jew would have anything to do; and yet it is the despised Samaritan who is the example to all, because he cared.

Still more is this, the case in the parable of the rich man and Lazarus (16:19-31). Day by day Lazarus, the poor man, was laid at the rich man's gate. The rich man was not consciously or deliberately cruel to Lazarus; he did not order him to be removed; he allowed him to have the crumbs that fell from his table. His trouble was that he never noticed Lazarus; he simply accepted Lazarus as part of the landscape; he did not for one moment think that the sufferings of Lazarus had anything to do with him. And then the scene changes and the poor man is in heaven and the rich man is in hell. As Hugh Martin says, it was not what the rich man did that got him into trouble; it was what he did not do that got him into hell. He had no concern, and so he found no mercy.

So the first question is quite simply, Do you care? Are you concerned for others? Or are you the unconcerned spectator who passes by on the other side?

ii. The second lesson which Luke presses home is that *we must get our values right*. He does this in the parable of the rich fool (12:13-20), and the parable of the unjust steward (16:1-9).

The first of these parables tells of the man who thought that, because he had amassed a goodly store of this world's goods, he was safe. He forgot that, when the end came, he could not take them with him, and that there were things — and character is one of them — which money cannot buy. No one is saying that material things do not make a difference. There is an old Scots saying: "Sorrow is not so sore where there is a loaf of bread." And to have enough is to have some at least of the worries of life lifted from our shoulders; but there comes an end, and in the end it is the things of the spirit that matter. The other story tells of a clever rascal who made use of all his skill and ingenuity and of all his chances to make life as comfortable as possible for himself, when the crash came. This story is saying to us: "If only men would make as much effort in their Christian life as they do in their material life, what a difference it would make!" If the Christian worked as hard at his religion as the business man does at his business, what a change there would be!

These two stories say to us: Have you got your

values right? Are you giving your strength and your effort to gain the things which really matter?

iii. The third piece of advice on which Luke insists is that, before we embark upon the Christian adventure, *we must count the cost.* If a man begins to build a tower and has to leave it half-finished, because he has failed to calculate the cost, he becomes nothing but a laughingstock. No king in his senses will embark upon a war before estimating his own resources and the resources of his opponent (14:28-32).

This is something on which Jesus always insists. Discipleship, he says, means the way of self-denial and of the Cross, as if to say: Think of that before you start (Luke 9:23-25). In the first flush of enthusiasm a man says that he will follow Jesus. Jesus' answer is that the foxes have their lairs and the birds have their nests, but he has nowhere to lay his head, again as if to say: Think of that before you start (Luke 9:58).

There is a kind of evangelism which seems to say: "Accept Jesus and his way, and you will have rest and peace and joy." In the sense that we have peace with God that is true, but the man who sets out on the Christian way will have a war to wage with sin and self; he will have standards to reach that he never had before; he will be pledged to a self-giving and a self-spending which will leave him exhausted. Luke faces the Christian convert and the Christian disciple with the demand: Have you counted the cost?

iv. It is Luke's insistence that the Christian must regard himself as a *man in debt*. The greater the forgiveness, the greater the love (7:40-43). The man who is accepted before God is not the man who thanks God that he is not as other men are, but the man who recognizes that in the eyes of God he is a sinner (18:9-14). How can the imperfection of man ever satisfy the perfection of God? How can the impurity of man stand before the holiness of God? How can the creature ever enter into the presence of the Creator? He cannot except through the life and death of Jesus Christ. It cost the life and death of Jesus Christ to open the way for us to God. We are eternally in his debt. So there comes the question: Have you realized what you cost? Have you realized that he died that we might live?

v. It is Luke's warning that *uselessness invites disaster*. The fig tree will be given every chance, but if in the end it still bears no fruit, it cannot go on taking all and giving nothing; it must be destroyed (Luke 13:6-9).

As Paul Tournier sees it, there are three essentials in life: "A man must live and work so as to respond to the divine claim made upon him." God has something for every man to do. Second, he must by meditation find out what that something is. "Meditation is the trusting and attentive attitude of waiting." Only by waiting do we find out the task which is ours. Thirdly, a man must find out the place where he can do and be what God means him to do and be. "The important thing for every man is not only to find a place, but to find his own true place, the one God wills for him."

We have a God-given task to do whether that task be in a kitchen or a palace, whether it be something that all men will see or something of which no one will know. To do it is the way to glory; to refuse it is the way to disaster. So the question comes: Am I in life for what I can put into it, or for what I can get out of it? Am I in life for my sake or for the sake of God and my fellowmen?

70

vi. Luke shows Jesus laying down the principle of *the inadequacy of the idea of duty*. When a servant has done his duty, he deserves no special credit for it; he has done only what he ought to do (17:7-10). The Christian motive is not duty; it is love. The person who thinks in terms of duty think in terms of that which an external compulsion can compel him to do; the person who thinks in terms of love knows no compulsion but that of the heart. The person who thinks in terms of duty thinks how little he can do; the person who thinks in terms of love can never do enough.

So we are compelled to ask: Do I think in terms of duty, or do I think in terms of love? Do I think in terms of the irreducible minimum of service, or in terms of the love which knows that to give God everything is still not to give enough?

vii. Above all Luke stresses *the seeking and the searching love of God*. This is this theme of the stories of the lost coin and the lost son (15:8-10; 11-32). A great Jewish scholar has said that these two stories have in them the very essence of Christianity, the new thing. It would be possible to find in Judaism the idea of a God who would take back the sinner who returned penitently and humbly to him; but nowhere is there the idea of a God who himself went out to look for the lost one in order to bring him home.

The coin *was* lost; it was lost not of its own fault but because someone took it and left it in the wrong place. The son *went* lost deliberately, of his own freewill, he left the father and went away to the far country. It does not matter whether a person is lost through someone else's fault or lost through no one's fault but his own, God in Jesus Christ seeks and finds. And the missioner of Jesus Christ must have that same passion to find the lost and to bring him home — no matter what the cost. F. W. Myers pictures Paul looking at the heathen world, bound by its sin, confronted by the offer of the seeking Christ:

> Only I see the folk thereunder,
>> Bound who should conquer, slaves who
>> should be kings,
> Hearing their own hope with an empty
>> wonder,
>> Sadly contented with a show of things.
> Then with a thrill the intolerable craving
>> Shivers throughout me like a trumpet call;

O to save these, to perish for their saving,
  Die for their life, be offered to them all.

So there comes to the Christian missioner the question: Do you love men as God loves them? Will you seek the lost as he sought them?

Do you care? Have you got your values right? Have you counted the cost of following Christ? Have you realized what you cost? Are you in life for what you can get out of it, or for what you can put into it? Do you think in terms of duty, or of love? Have you God's own passion to bring home the souls of men? These are the questions with which Luke confronts the Christian missioner.

For Discussion

1. What does it mean really to care? What kind of action will real caring issue in?

2. What is the cost of following Jesus? What is the price of true Christian loyalty?

3. Wherein does doing one's duty fall short of the ideal of the Christian way of life?

4. What does it mean to have a passion for the souls of men? How will that passion be expressed?

Notes

7

THE END AND THE BEGINNING

The cross came as no surprise to Jesus. From the beginning of his life to the end of his life he knew that it was coming. All through his life we can trace his consciousness of the cross.

(a) God's voice came to Jesus at his baptism, "Thou are my beloved Son; with thee I am well pleased" (Luke 3:22). That is a composite quotation from the Old Testament. "Thou are my Beloved Son" is Psalm 2:7 and Psalm 2 is a coronation Psalm which tells of the enthroning and the triumph of the king. "With thee I am well pleased" is a quotation of Isaiah 42:1, a passage which refers to the Servant, whose portrait is most vividly drawn in Isaiah 53, and who was "wounded for our transgressions and bruised for our iniquities" (Isaiah 53:5). Right from the beginning Jesus knew that he was king, but he knew that that kingship was not to be expressed in the power and the glory but in the sacrifical way of love.

(b) Very soon the orthodox were to say of Jesus that he and his disciples were far too happy. He asked them how the wedding guests could fail to be happy when the bridegroom was with them. And then there comes the saying: "The day will come when the bridegroom is taken away from them, and then they will fast in those days" (Luke 5:33-35). Jesus was the bridegroom, and from the beginning he knew that there would come a day, when the bridegroom would be killed.

(c) We might say that in Luke's story these are still only hints, below the surface, clear to Jesus but not realized by anyone else. But, as Luke has it, there comes the open assertion that he was on the way to death. No sooner has Peter

77

made his great affirmation that Jesus is the Messiah than Jesus warned him: "The Son of Man must suffer many things, and be rejected by the elders and chief priests and scribes, and be killed and on the third day rise again." (Luke 9:18-22) Openly he told me of the end.

(d) Not long afterwards in Luke's story another note enters in. After the incident of the Transfiguration and of the healing of the epileptic boy, Jesus said: "Let these words sink into your ears; for the Son of Man is to be delivered into the hands of men." And then Luke goes on to say that the disciples did not know what Jesus meant, and that they were afraid to ask him (Luke 9:43-45). Jesus had begun clearly to tell men that he was on the way to the cross, and they were quite unable to grasp what he was saying, and this inability continued.

(e) When he set out for Jerusalem on the last journey, it was "to be received up" (Luke 9:51). Jesus was never in any doubt about what awaited him at the end of the journey. So he set out for

Jerusalem, "for it cannot be that a prophet should perish away from Jerusalem" (13:33) Open eyed he took the martyr's road.

(f) And then still another note enters into it. He took the Twelve and told them: "Behold, we are going up to Jerusalem, and everything that is written of the Son of Man by the prophets will be accomplished; for he will be delivered to the Gentiles, and will be mocked and shamefully treated and spit upon; they will scourge him and kill him, and on the third day he will rise." (Luke 19:31-34) The new note is that Jesus was going not to death but to destiny. Here was no sudden emergency situation; it was something in which the will of God was being worked out, and in which the message of the prophets was coming true. "The Son of Man goes as it has been determined." (Luke 22:22) "I tell you that this scripture must be fulfilled in me. And he was reckoned with the transgressors; for what is written about me has its fulfillment." (Luke 22:37)

Things were not out of control; the will of God was being worked out, that will which in Gethsemane Jesus accepted (Luke 22:42).

(g) Lastly, there is the parable of the wicked husbandman which Jesus told in the last days (Luke 20:9-18), in which he makes it quite clear that he knows that the son is going to be violently killed, and in which the fate of his murderers is clearly stated, a parable of which, as Luke tells the story, the hearers clearly saw the meaning, and were horrified (Luke 20:15, 16). From the moment Jesus began his ministry until the end came in tragedy, Jesus was never in any doubt that he was going to die, and he was never in any doubt that, although his death was the crime of man, it was nevertheless the will of God and his own destiny.

What then was Jesus doing in these last days within the shadow of the cross? The prophets of the Old Testament had a special way of getting their message across. It is called dramatic prophetic action. When words had no effect, when people apparently would not listen to or heed words, then the prophet *did* something, something sensational, vivid and dramatic. Ahijah the prophet saw that Rehoboam was going to lose the kingdom, and that the main body of the people were going to go over to Jeroboam. He put on a new robe; he went out and met Jeroboam. He tore off the robe and ripped it into twelve pieces. Ten of the pieces he handed to Jeroboam and two he kept. He thus showed dramatically that ten of the tribes were going to revolt to Jeroboam and only two would remain faithful to Rehoboam (1 Kings 11:26-40). When Jeremiah wished to compel people to see that the coming conquests by Nebuchadnezzar were inevitable, he went about wearing yoke-bars and thongs (Jeremiah 27). Ezekiel constantly used this means of compelling people to pay attention (Ezekiel 4).

Towards the close of his ministry Jesus repeatedly used dramatic prophetic action. This is what he did when he came riding into Jerusalem at what we call the Triumphal Entry (Luke 19:28-40). Make no mistake as to what this incident means. In the east the ass was not the despised donkey of the west; the ass was a handsome and noble animal, and it was the animal on which kings rode, when they came in peace; they rode on horses only when riding to war. And so at the Triumphal Entry Jesus made his appeal to men. In dramatic prophetic action more vivid than words he was saying: "Will you take me as your king, not the warrior king, but the king who comes to you in peace?"

When he ate with his men for the last time (Luke 22:14-20), he was saying in dramatic prophetic action: "Look! Just as this bread is broken, my body is going to be broken — for you. Look! Just as this scarlet wine is poured out, my red life-blood is going to be poured out — for you." In action more dramatic than words he was compelling men to look; he was rivetting their attention on himself.

And the supreme dramatic action is the cross

(Luke 23:24-49). On the cross Jesus was dramatically saying two things: He was saying: "Look! See what sin can do — sin can take the loveliest life that was ever lived and smash it on this cross. Sin is the most destructive thing in all the universe." But he was also saying: "Look! See what love can do. You do this — and I still love you. You crucify me in agony and I pray for your forgiveness. I love you like that!" On the cross there is shown vividly and dramatically the length to which man's sin will go and the length to which God's love will go.

But the cross was not the end. If the cross had been the end, it might have been possible to say that sin had won. After the cross there came the Resurrection, and the Resurrection is the proof that not all that man can do can kill the love of God, that the love of God is not only sacrificial; it is triumphant. It not only suffers; it conquers. It not only dies; it vanquishes death for evermore.

So the Risen Christ said two things to his disciples. First, he said to them that all history had been leading up to him (Luke 24:25-27; 44-47). Second, he said that what happened on the cross is designed to awaken penitence and to make the forgiveness of God available to men. And so, he said, his men must wait until the power of the Holy Spirit came upon them, and then they must go out to preach the suffering and the conquering love of God, and to witness to what that love in Jesus Christ had done for them.

We are the descendants of those first disciples. We too must look at the cross. We too must realize that it was for us he hung and suffered there. Our hearts too must be broken in penitence and flooded with forgiveness. We too must be clothed with the Holy Spirit. And we too in our day and generation must go out to bring the love of God to men and to bring men to the love of God, for that is what evangelism means.

For Discussion

1. Think specially of the courage of Jesus. It is brave to do the heroic thing on the reaction of the moment. But it takes a still higher courage to see the end long and far in advance, and to go on. Are there any special threats and dangers which the evangelist must see, and yet refuse to allow them to deflect him?

2. Do we preach the Resurrection enough? Is it true that the preaching of the Resurrection is very largely confined to Easter Sunday? For the early preachers the Resurrection was the center of every sermon they preached (Acts 2:24; 3:15; 4:10; 5:31; 13:30; 17:31). Do we tend to stop at the cross? Ought we to rediscover the Resurrection, and to remember that we worship one who is not only a crucified Savior but who is also the risen Lord?

3. It is said that the church has never had an "official" theory of the Atonement. Think out what happened on the cross, and in your thinking beware of that intolerance which will allow no view but its own.

Notes

Bibliography

For those who wish to undertake further and more detailed study there is ample material. For those who can use the Greek text there are commentaries by A. B. Bruce in the *Expositor's Greek Testament;* by A. Plummer in the *International Critical Commentary;* and by J. M. Creed in the *Macmillan Commentary.*

There are commentaries on the English text by W. M. Manson in the *Moffatt Commentary;* by A. R. C. Leaney in the *A. and C. Black Commentary;* by G. B. Caird in the *Pelican Commentary;* by E. Earle Ellis in the *New Century Bible;* and by myself in the *Daily Study Bible.*

There is material about Luke's Gospel in general in the New Testament Introductions such as F. C. Grant's *The Gospels;* R. M. Grant's *Historical Introduction to the New Testament;* A. M. Hunter's *Introducing the New Testament;* E. B. Red-lich's *Students' Introduction to the Synoptic Gospels;* E. F. Scott's *Literature of the New Testament;* Vincent Taylor's *The Gospels.*

There are special studies such as C. K. Barrett's *Luke the Historian in Recent Study* and H. Con-zelmann's *The Theology of St. Luke.*